The Working Mom's Survival Guide

JAYNE GARRISON

POCKET GUIDES
Tyndale House Publishers, Inc.
Wheaton, Illinois

Dedicated to the memory of Kathleen Souer

Adapted from *The Christian Working Mother's Handbook,* copyright 1986 by Jayne Garrison. Published by Tyndale House Publishers, Inc.

Chapter 10, copyright April 1988 by Ruth Senter.

Library of Congress Catalog Card Number 88-50921
ISBN 0-8423-8397-2

95   94   93   92   91
  6   5   4   3   2

CONTENTS

The Basic Concern: Child Care

I met up with Karen at the central copy machine one day at work. Heavy with child, she was due for maternity leave at the end of the week.

"What about child care?" I asked inquisitively. "Have you got it all set up?"

Karen looked startled.

"No," she said. "There are so many little kids in our neighborhood, and everybody works—so, I just don't see baby-sitting as a big deal. I mean, all of those kids have to be taken care of by someone!"

Some time later, Karen had the baby and returned to work after the appropriate six-week interval. And, sure enough, life had turned out to be blissfully easy—the woman next door was caring for little John. I was almost jealous, remembering all the sitters and child-care centers I'd gone through in the past years . . . and none of them next door!

But a few weeks later, Karen joined the rest of us in the real world. It seemed her neighbor no longer wanted to keep an infant.

"Now what do I do?" I overheard her tearfully asking another woman.

"You worry a lot," the woman answered dryly.

Karen smiled through her tears. But I didn't. For in truth, the woman had spoken volumes. Child-care arrangements are probably the working mother's number one concern. So important is the relationship between a satisfactory child-care arrangement and a woman's job performance that finding child care should be approached as seriously as the job hunt itself.

Where does one look for competent, affordable child care? A lot will depend upon geographic location and income. For instance, those New York City nannies sound terribly good to those of us in the Midwest, but not at all realistic. They'd require more than half of our salary! Nor does suburban life help matters. What with its lack of public transportation, we even have a difficult time enticing the younger and older women from our area to come out each day. So, we usually do a lot of "asking around," following hunches, and reading between the lines. Sound familiar? If so, here are a few important considerations to help you base your child-care decision on sound, reasonable expectations.

KNOW YOUR ALTERNATIVES

The choice is not strictly between expensive nannies and budget child-care centers. Investigate every option in your area—carefully weighing the pros and cons of each.

Mother's helper—A good answer for the part-time employee. These women usually don't want to work full time but will often do light housework as well as look after your child. To find such a person, advertise in a college newspaper or the local shopper. You'll probably discover she's willing to accept minimum wage or less.

Relatives—Grandparents make especially wonderful caretakers *if* they're available. Besides, their services are usually free, and grandparents can give your child a keen sense of security. To avoid friction, you must be willing to relinquish your child during these hours—advice easier given than done, particularly if you're depending upon in-laws who may do things very differently from you.

Baby-sitter—Baby-sitters are most often found through local newspapers or by word of mouth. Those who require you to bring your child to their house will usually be priced a little under the going day-care center rate. If you must have someone in your home, be prepared to pay a great deal more. However, you can be creative in how you meet this expense. One woman I know shares her baby-sitter with the woman next door. One week the baby-sitter comes to my friend's house and the neighbor brings her child over. The next week, the arrangement is reversed.

Probably the most crucial problem in dealing with private baby-sitters is lack of dependability. To encourage regular service whether in your home or hers, pay your sitter a tad more than average and offer a bonus for "no days missed."

Role reversal—Daddy takes on the traditional responsibilities of Mom under this plan. It seems to work well when the husband's occupation can be home-based or when the wife has the higher income potential. For a child to get to know his father in such an intimate way is a rare and wonderful privilege.

Work co-op—Part-time working moms can form a baby-sitting co-op arranged around their various working schedules. This requires a fairly large network of friends, though participants could probably be found through advertising in a local newspaper.

Commercial or church day-care centers—Both should be judged by the same criteria. And neither need be feared strictly on the basis of adverse publicity. Common sense and a watchful eye can help keep your child safe in a day-care setting.

HOW TO CHOOSE THE BEST

Choosing the right center in the first place is a big advantage. Although you shouldn't hesitate for a moment about withdrawing your child from a suspicious environment, remember that frequent day-care hopping is hard on the child. If finding the right place is taking longer than you expected, contact your future employer and request another week before coming to work. You don't have to say why—something about taking care of business matters will suffice.

To help you make your decision, here are some simple guidelines to follow. Check for:

1. Clean, spacious playrooms.
2. Fenced playgrounds with climbing equipment.
3. Nutritious lunches.
4. A cot and blanket for each child.
5. A teacher for every eighteen children.
6. A safe environment—with no ungated stairways, open doors to the street, or accessible cleaning agents.
7. A willingness by the staff to show you around at any time. While it's true the director may need to make an appointment with you to discuss fees, your request to look around the premises should be pleasantly honored. Closed doors or "forbidden" areas are red flags. (The least you can expect to find behind them is hidden filth.)

Ideally, a day-care teacher should be affectionate, articulate, patient, creative, and enthusiastic. But what it really boils down to is that few day-care centers pay enough to attract such people. You'll have to be willing to compensate by providing lots of extra attention at home. One way to know whether you've made the right decision is by observing how eager your child is to leave each morning.

Day-care Dos and Don'ts

You *can* help your child adjust to the new day-care situation. Here are some pointers.

1. Try out the arrangement before you begin work. Start part time and build up to full days.
2. Provide your child with a link to home, such as a blanket or a toy.
3. Arrive fifteen minutes early in the morning. This prevents the feeling of being hurriedly dumped, and helps your child get reoriented to his daytime environment.
4. Help your child make a special friend by inviting another child from the center to play at your house on the weekend.
5. Watch for signs of extreme distress: excessive crying or clinging, reverting to immature behavior, bed-wetting, etc.
6. Never threaten to leave your child at the center as punishment.
7. Always be on time for evening pickup. Try to come early every once in a while.
8. To ensure that all is well, make periodic unexpected visits.
9. Day-care needs change as a child grows. Young children need physical care, older children, a sense of companionship. Involve older children in after-school activities—volunteer work, baby-sitting, music or drama lessons, and so forth.

CHAPTER 2

Keeping in Touch with Your Family

I often think the most difficult part of being a working mother is the feeling of isolation from one's children. Living in a large metropolitan area can tend to exaggerate this feeling. Every morning my husband leaves for a city thirty miles to the west, I leave for a city thirty miles to the east, and our daughter goes across town to her school—each one of us is in a different town all day long. So often I am struck with the thought that I haven't the vaguest idea what's going on in my family's world—particularly my daughter's. What if she needs me? For though I've instructed her teacher time and again to feel free to call me at work, I know she wouldn't want to call for something trivial.

Touch is important to children. But because we working mothers can't reach out and actually stroke our youngsters during the day, we need to discover other ways to give them a sense of security and well-being.

SAY IT WITH A NOTE

One way to do this is through note writing. We write a lot of notes in my family. Periodically I'll put a note in my daughter's lunch kit. Sometimes it's a short confirmation of love.

Dear Heather, You're my daughter, and I love you.—Mama

Another time I may clip a puzzle from the newspaper and suggest that she complete it after school. And at still other times, I may put together a praise letter, glorifying some small act of goodness she has performed.

Heather looks forward to these lunchtime notes. They are her contact with Mama in the middle of a long, hard day. For that reason alone, notes are important. But they may also be an effective way to elicit cooperation in household chores.

If Heather and her father are going to get home before me, I often leave a note explaining that I expect the living area to be tidied or the dinner started. Somehow, a written note seems more official than a hurriedly spoken request.

Of course, it's a nice touch to leave instructions for a fun activity every once in a while. I sometimes suggest in a note that Heather play a board game with a neighbor or make herself a banana sandwich. The spontaneity of these notes makes them more valuable.

Note writing is also a good way to keep close tabs on your child's school progress. When Heather entered the first grade, she would invariably come forward with an arm full of papers just as I was about to start supper, load the washing machine, or straighten the living area. The result was usually a hurried, "Why, that's wonderful, dear."

Then one day I hit upon the idea of taking her papers with me to work and regrading them according to my own scale. Heather was delighted. And so was I, when I sat down at break to a cup of coffee and the wonder of my child's expanding knowledge. On each paper I wrote a note—"good idea," "I like these colors," "great work," and so on.

This plan met with such enthusiasm from Heather that it is now the regular procedure at our house for parental feedback on school-work.

CREATIVE COMMUNICATION

Communicating with older children creates an even greater challenge, for each year you'll find less and less information being revealed to you through conversation. This is true even when Mom doesn't work, but the problem is compounded when she doesn't get home before 6:00 or 7:00 P.M.

For one thing, children are most likely to talk about their day immediately after getting home. By the time a working mom arrives on the scene, homework, television, and maybe even neighborhood activity take precedence over what happened several hours ago. Then, too, older children often sense how tired and hurried their working mother is and decide that it's wiser not to get underfoot.

So, one of the best ways for us to find out what's going on in the lives of these children is to ask questions—open-ended ones that require more than a yes or no answer. Examples: "What did you do in math today?" "What kinds of questions were on your English test?" "What are you studying in history?" But remember—when your child begins to talk—be ready to listen! Actually stop what you're doing and make eye contact. Then, accept what is said, even though you may not like what you hear.

Since most teenagers like talking on the telephone, this could be a very effective way to establish conversational rapport with your older child. Try calling home each afternoon during your break for a quick chat. But avoid leaving the impression of "checking up" or calling to give orders.

When you must give instructions *in absentia,* do so in an interesting, nonoffensive manner. For instance, a cartoon related to a controversial family rule, taped in a prominent place, may seem more friendly than a verbal reminder to obey the rule.

To get the conversation flowing back to you, introduce the "talk box." Place a decorated shoe box with a slit in the top in a busy traffic area. Invite your children to write everything from grievances to grocery needs on a slip of paper and insert it in the box.

Permission slips, report cards, and other school notes can also be put in the box. After checking the box each night, you should be up on your household's daily affairs.

If older teens balk at the "talk box" approach, you may prefer to instigate a doodle pad. In the book *Get It All Done and Still Be Human* by Tony and Robbie Fanning, one woman said she taped a sheet of blank newsprint to the entire top of a telephone desk and placed a can of colored markers on the desk. Messages, reminders, ideas, gripes, and unusual doodles soon filled up the page—at which time she merely replaced the old with a new. One of the sheets was so interesting and typified the family's life-style so well that she had it framed and hung over the desk.

Another woman has found early morning the best time for making contact with her teenage son. She likes to eat breakfast with him and then continue their visit as she drives him to school. This is a nice way of ensuring your child a good start each day. But if neither of you is a morning person, you can reserve Saturday mornings for a late breakfast at an inexpensive coffee shop. If there is more than one older child in the family, alternate between taking all the children and taking one at a time.

Families who are able to come together each night, but not necessarily at dinner time, might like to try the after-dinner dessert plan. Instead of offering dessert at the end of the meal, serve a dessert in the middle of the evening as a homework/family-time break.

THE FAMILY COUNCIL

But probably one of the very best ways to communicate within the family is the family council. This solution for coming together as a family works with any number or age of children and can even be effective when parents are divorced—provided communication channels are still open.

Just what is a family council? It is simply a regularly scheduled meeting during which all members of the family meet and discuss anything they like. Each member is encouraged to present his opinion. And while parents should not allow children to carry out suggestions that would endanger their health or welfare, in these meetings, a child's opinion is as important as Mom's or Dad's. For example, maybe a child would like to have a slumber party, but Mom feels the child is too young. A discussion during family council might result in a compromise, allowing the child to invite one friend to sleep over.

Other topics usually discussed in a family council include recreation, disagreements, family rules, finances, and the sharing of household duties. A meeting is not, however, to become an ordinary gripe session.

There are several advantages to the family council. Not only does it lift the burden of decision making off a single parent, but it eliminates arguing during the week—everyone knows that the opportunity to discuss the problem will be made fairly and sensitively. Then, too, children learn within the council that their views and feelings are important to the entire family—that each person is a valued part of a whole.

How to Start a Family Council
1. Discuss the theory of a council with your family.
2. Agree to a place and time of meeting.
3. Decide on a chairperson democratically.
4. Discuss rules for the family council.
5. Select a secretary to record discussions and decisions.

Make the meetings fun. You might, for instance, illustrate the problem under discussion with a simple cartoon drawn on poster board. Then ask the children what they would do if they were in the cartoon. Another time you might ask family members to write their solutions to a problem on paper and submit them to the chairperson anonymously. Perhaps an opinion poll taken during the week by your secretary could be a useful tool in making a decision. Or you may want to introduce role-playing as a means of discovering new insights. There are so many exciting, creative opportunities in these meetings. One suggestion, however: Begin with a prayer and end with special refreshments.

No one should be required to attend family council, but attendance is encouraged by the fact that decisions can be made about absent members. If you encourage an atmosphere of openness and fluidity, however, your council will be cheerfully and eagerly anticipated.

TAKING TIME FOR TOGETHERNESS
Sometimes the communication void in a two-career family is between husband and wife. How does one improve or even maintain a successful relationship when there is so little time for togetherness?

One couple says the telephone is their lifeline. "My husband travels," the wife relates. "Telephoning each other regularly and being open about plans has helped us reach a good level of sharing even when apart."

Attending each other's company functions is also an aid in maintaining communication. Knowing the people your spouse works with will make work-related conversations more meaningful and fun.

Writing notes can also work wonders between spouses. A note slipped into a briefcase that says, "I'll be praying about the 2:00 P.M. sales meeting" can be just the boost your spouse needs.

Occasionally, there will be problems or concerns in your family that need the full attention of both you and your husband. Don't cheat yourself out of a full discussion with a few terse words in front of the television. Schedule a time and place to meet at day's end to work through such problems without the interference of household demands.

Finally, create special events to celebrate the joy of being husband and wife. Candlelight dinners, late evening walks, stargazing on the front porch, and praying together before bedtime are just a few of the rituals that can bring couples together at the end of a very busy day.

DO YOU KNOW HOW TO LISTEN?

Some children just don't share their thoughts, or perhaps they're like my daughter and do so after the fact. A typical mother's response is, "But why didn't you tell me sooner?" The fact is, very often they have, but we were too busy to listen.

Dr. Joseph Novello gives some good pointers on listening in his book *Bringing Up Kids American Style*. He says, if you find yourself monopolizing conversation, stop and ask yourself who owns the conversation. The answer is: the first person who spoke. If it was the other person, your duty is to help him express himself until he indicates a new topic or throws the conversation back to you. If you interrupt with a new topic, you're guilty of robbing the other person of the conversation—and his self-esteem.

As you listen, determine the theme, feeling, and tone. Particularly with children, it's not always clear. Listen for not just *what* is said but *how* it is said. Keep the conversation going by asking questions, tilting your head in an attentive manner, or nodding with understanding. It's important to look at the person, to read body language, and to show through yours that you care.

Finally, help close the conversation in a positive way by saying, "Thanks for sharing," or "It was nice talking with you."

Morning Management

I don't like to admit it, but mornings can be completely transformed by setting the alarm a little earlier and then actually getting up when it rings. It's been my experience that mothers should rise at least one full hour before their family.

If you have trouble rising as early as you'd like, read on. These ideas may help you get off to a better start.

1. Plan ahead. Decide in the evening what you'd like to accomplish the next day. Like a business executive, you may even want to make a list. As you sleep, your subconscious mind will actually prepare you for the activities ahead.

2. Develop an evening routine.
   a. Insist upon all baths being taken before going to bed.
   b. Lay out the next day's clothing (this includes yours, your husband's, and the children's).
   c. Pick up the house.
   d. Write special notes to teachers.
   e. Pack school lunches and store in the refrigerator.

3. Place the alarm clock across the room from your bed so you will have to get up to turn it off. Keep a warm robe and slippers close by, however, so that you won't be tempted to return to the warmth of the bed.

4. Splash cool water or astringent on your face for a quick wake-up.

5. Establish a morning routine. Dress, eat a light breakfast, and spend at least fifteen minutes in prayer. This done, open the curtains to let in the sunshine, or turn on the lights to create a warm, cheerful atmosphere. Wake the children and your husband. As they are dressing, prepare a simple but nutritious breakfast. Spend a few minutes sharing in their day's plans. Then, if there's still time, make your bed.

I suppose anyone could be responsible for seeing that the family gets off to the right kind of start each day. But the point is, *someone* has to take the responsibility. If no one else in the family has slipped into this role, you can surely see the importance of taking on the job. As a mother, you can set the tone of the day and ensure that your family leaves a happy, love-filled home each morning. Certainly this is the kind of atmosphere your family is most likely to want to return to at the end of each day.

QUICK AND EASY BREAKFAST IDEAS
Hint: After washing dinner dishes, set the table for tomorrow's breakfast. Serve:
• Breakfast sandwiches: Split an English muf-

fin, add a fried egg and a slice of ham and
cheese. Heat in oven until cheese melts.
- Cheese toast, fruit, and milk
- Frozen pancakes, waffles, or French toast,
  and fruit juice
- Cinnamon toast, fruit, and milk
- Cold cereal, toast, and fruit juice
- Milkshakes

Banana Milkshake
1 cup milk
1 banana
½ tsp. vanilla extract
Mash banana, add milk, and blend in blender
on high. (You can also blend with a hand
beater or shake in a jar.) Serve at once.

If you own a microwave oven, don't forget
to use it to prepare scrambled or poached
eggs now and then. Though doctors no longer stress the "egg a day," and we're all looking out for cholesterol levels, we do know
that high protein foods seem to help school
children perform better on tests. Working
mothers don't always have time to prepare
eggs, but if you know your child is facing a
series of important tests, you may want to
rise earlier to prepare eggs. Another alterna-
tive would be stopping at a fast-food restaurant on the way to school and work.

COPING WITH MORNING
EMERGENCIES
A Mother's Law of Probability is "If some-
thing can go wrong—it will happen in the

morning while you're trying to get to work!"

Mornings are naturally a bit frantic for working moms—there's such a lot to do in so very little time. But what about those days when things are more hectic than usual—when something over which you have no control seems predestined to keep you from getting to work—period? Because situations like this are every working mother's nightmare, you'll feel more secure if you're just the slightest bit prepared for these mini-disasters. Follow this chart to get a jump on morning emergencies.

Emergency: The baby-sitter calls in sick.
Emergency Action: Here are your options:
1. Stay at home and miss a day of work.
2. Call someone from your alternate baby-sitter list.
3. Make an arrangement with your husband in which each of you takes a half-day child care responsibility. (Bosses generally appreciate this kind of effort.)
Preventive Action: Prepare a list of emergency baby-sitters. Your alternatives could include a drop-in service at a commercial day-care center, a call to a relative, or perhaps a stay-at-home mother who would be willing to baby-sit in emergency situations. Talk to each of these people ahead of time so that you can be certain of their availability.

Emergency: Your child is sick.
Emergency Action: If at all possible, stay at

home. Being sick is stressful enough without the administrations of a stranger or the trauma of being carted across town to Grandma's house. However, if there's a crucial reason for your not missing work, you can again share "home" duty with your husband. Some cities have the unique service of home baby-sitting for sick children. However, these services are usually expensive and best suited for the professional woman who simply mustn't take time away from the office.

Emergency: You awake to no electricity.
Emergency Action: Grab a flashlight and check the circuit box. If this doesn't bring results, telephone the electric company to find out if the problem is area-wide and how long you should expect to be without power. While speaking with the electric company's representative, you might ask for the time—particularly if your household is run by an electric clock. Since you may have overslept, make a note to telephone your boss of your probable late arrival.

You won't have use of your hair dryer, and assuming the power failure is throughout the neighborhood, you can't run next door. So don't wash you hair. Instead, pat a cotton ball soaked in witch hazel on your scalp. Then brush baby powder or corn starch through your hair. A pretty comb or headband will complete your emergency hairstyle.

Feed your family a cold cereal breakfast, and depending upon the amount of time you expect your power will be off, consider carrying your frozen goods to a friend's house for the day.

Preventive Action: Select a hairstyle that is either short enough to air dry on occasion or long enough to pin up. Keep witch hazel and baby powder in the bathroom cabinet. If there are frequent power failures in your area, purchase a hand-wound alarm clock and a large ice chest for storage of frozen goods. Other helpful measures include keeping a flashlight near your bed and candles and matches in the kitchen.

Emergency: You awake to no water.

Emergency Action: If there are very young children in the family, you may have to consider missing the first half of your work day. In that case, you need to telephone your boss to inform him of your crisis. Next, contact the water department. Chances are, repair work is being done in your area, and you'll have water again in a few hours. In the meantime, you need to locate a water supply. If you have a baby for whom you need water to prepare formula or other food, you'll need to carry some containers to the nearest gas station and bring some water home.

Preventive Action: Keep a bottle of drinking water in the refrigerator, and try to keep a few cans of prepared formula on hand for feeding the baby in emergency situations.

Emergency: Your car won't start.

Emergency Action: If it looks like it's the

car's battery, call your husband, who may already be at work, a friend, a relative, or as a last resort, a service station that makes service calls. Then notify your boss that you'll be late. In the event that the problem can't be quickly corrected, and you simply must be at work for an important meeting, call a cab.

Once at work, you can use the telephone to make further arrangements for your car's repair. Someone in your office will probably even be willing to give you a ride home.

Preventive Action: Join an auto club that makes service calls—especially if your husband travels and you're on your own most of the week. It's also a good idea to locate a reliable private mechanic. You'll find the private garage owner more willing to work around your schedule than a large chain-operated one.

In addition, keep a pair of jumper cables in your car trunk and the phone numbers of all potential helpers in your personal telephone directory. If change is a problem, it's a wise idea to keep taxi money in a special emergency kitty.

Emergency: At the last minute you notice that your hem's out, and you have to meet with the company president, first thing.

Emergency Action: Staple or tape your hem in place. Once back at your desk, repair with the sewing kit that you keep in your drawer.

Emergency: You're out of toothpaste and mouthwash.

Emergency Action: Brush your teeth with baking soda. Rinse mouth well with water.

Emergency: You've broken a nail and can't find a nail file.
Emergency Action: Use the striking portion of a matchbook to smooth the broken edge of your nail.

Emergency: A personal problem causes you to cry just before leaving for work. Your eyes are swollen and red.
Emergency Action: Soak tea bags in cold water, place them on your eyes, and rest for a few minutes. Then, with your finger, apply cream coverstick around eyes and nose. Cover area with pressed powder and press a wrung-out damp tissue over face to freshen makeup.

Emergency: You're only days away from making a presentation—and a big blemish appears on your face.
Emergency Action: Rub a styptic pencil (used on razor cuts) on the pimple three times a day. It will quickly dry up.

Emergency: You've run your last pair of pantyhose.
Emergency Action: Cut the damaged leg off pantyhose and match it with another one-legged pair. At your first free moment at work, exchange your makeshift stockings for the emergency pair you keep in your desk drawer.

Emergency: The children announce they haven't any clean socks.
Emergency Action: Turn their cleanest pair inside out, and promise yourself that in the future you will check on these things before going to bed.

Emergency: Your hair is responding to the weather in frizzy, flyaway fashion.
Emergency Action: Rub a fabric-softener sheet through your hair for a taming effect.

Organization: Setting Things Straight

Regardless of their trade, I've found professional women to have this in common: Our work makes us feel more whole—a fact we've come to know and accept. It also takes an immense toll on our family—in ways we neither know nor accept.

Let's face it. If we choose to combine a career with homemaking, our lives cannot realistically run as smoothly or calmly as those of traditional homemakers. But one way to minimize the adverse effects of a double calling is to be supremely organized.

Organized people have a clear perception of their environment, have surrounded themselves with tools for effective living, and know how to find these tools when needed.

A NOTEBOOK— WOMAN'S BEST FRIEND

First step: Find a notebook, preferably an attractive fabric or leather one that you plan to keep. Make sure it will fit into your purse but is large enough to write in. Henceforth it should be with you at all times.

What should go into your notebook? Anything that comes to you throughout the day. Laundry tickets, birthday presents, recipes, prayer requests, and so on. This is your personal data bank. Use your notebook to plan ahead. Before going to bed, decide what you hope to accomplish the next day and write it in your notebook. Most important, don't just write in your notebook—remember periodically to browse through it! Check on your progress by marking off the duties you've accomplished.

Think you'll join me in my efforts toward attaining order? Congratulations! You have just become a coordinator of life.

HELPFUL HINTS
1. Schedule everything—even the fun things such as eating out and family birthday parties.
2. Keep a spare set of car keys in a safe place so that if you happen to misplace yours, you can look for them at leisure.
3. Patronize shops such as cleaners and repair shops near your home or place of business.
4. Hang a big calendar in the kitchen. Fill in all appointments, birthdays, and other scheduled events.
5. Learn to say no without forgetting when to say yes.

6. Establish a family communication center for leaving notes.
7. Give yourself some peace and quiet time.
8. Develop a reading file. When a magazine arrives via the mail, spend a short time tearing out articles you want to read; discard the rest. Put the articles in a folder that you can carry with you and read during "waiting" moments. Put interesting but not urgent reading into a trip folder—designated for reading on your next trip. Throw away the articles or pass them on to a friend after you've read them.
9. Make a habit of writing dates on things as you put them away. This includes business cards, notes, and clippings.
10. Don't save junk. Sell it in a garage sale or give it to the children to play with for a while—then throw it out!
11. When reading correspondence, underline in red ink the questions you'll need to answer by return mail.

MAKE A LIST

Lists are a key to organization. Don't stop with a grocery list; incorporate this type of planning into every area of your life.

Here are a few lists you may want to start keeping.

1. A shopping list—Keep this ongoing list in your purse or on your kitchen counter. Add to it the minute you think of something you'll need from the grocery on your next stop.

2. A menu list—Make this before going to the grocery store. After shopping, tape it to one of your kitchen cabinets so there'll be no confusion as to "what's for dinner."

3. A gift list—As they come to you, jot down appropriate gift ideas for various family members. When Christmas or birthdays arrive, you'll have only to check your list for that perfect gift!

4. A Christmas card list—And while you're at it, why not a regular correspondence list?

5. A prayer list—Write your prayer requests and cross them out as each one is met.

6. A book list—Keep a record of books you'd like to read. You'll find trips to the library more profitable when you know what type of book you're looking for.

7. A "to-do" list—Before going to bed at night, plan for the day ahead. List the things you'd like to accomplish the next day. Mark the jobs of top priority.

8. A "things I'd like to do" list—On this list you may write anything from eating ice cream to planting rosebushes. When you're going through a blue spell, this list can serve as a true spirit lifter. Make it a point to do something on this list regularly.

KEEPING HOUSE AND A
BUSY LIFE TO BOOT

Since you're an active woman, you need to be extra efficient with your housecleaning time. Here are a few ways of effectively managing this responsibility.

1. Hire outside help at least once a month. Yes, it is possible for just about anyone. Teenagers will often work for a reduced rate just to get steady work, while housewives may be willing to clean your home in exchange for another service. *Between paid housecleaning jobs:*

    a. Pick up clutter each evening before going to bed.

    b. Use a feather duster for quick touch-ups in the living area.

    c. Run your dishwasher after you've gone to bed. Put away clean dishes the next day while you prepare the evening meal.

    d. Wash the tub during your bath time.

    e. Keep a bottle of rubbing alcohol in the bathroom. A small amount on a piece of tissue will clean your vanity and sink in seconds.

    f. Clean the refrigerator as you put away groceries.

    g. Train your family to put away or clean up as they go.

    h. Place a basket by the door for gloves, scarves, and hats.

    i. Add a thirty-foot extension cord to your vacuum cleaner, and you'll save yourself the trouble of stopping and starting.

    j. Purchase an extra-long telephone cord or strategically place the kitchen phone so that you can continue cleaning up while talking.

    k. Solve the laundry sorting problem

by purchasing dishpans for each member of the family's clean clothes and labeling them with each person's name. Instruct family members to collect and put away their own clothing.

2. Bonnie McCullough, a personal and home management consultant, suggests the simple technique of decluttering the home as an effective housecleaning measure. Based on the theory that clutter creates the illusion of dirt, her procedure involves spending five minutes a day per room for general pickup. Bonnie's advice? Begin where your efforts will show the most. Pick up large items such as cushions first, and work your way down to the smaller items that can be placed in a basket as you go.

3. Ever wonder how to get the family to help with housekeeping chores? Begin thinking of yourself as a working family, not just a working mother.

Your children stand to benefit in many ways from your work. Author David Melton (*Survival Kit for Parents of Teenagers*) believes the benefits should be explained to your teenager in detail. Perhaps it would do just as well to extend his suggestion to all family members. Children need to know that braces, a nice wardrobe, cheerleader fees, or the new bicycle are available partly because Mom works.

Melton suggests discussing these benefits at a family meal and then explaining the duties of each person in order for the working situation to succeed—laundry, simple dinner preparation, and so on. He says to give your child a realistic allowance that's worth working for. Then, for each job not completed, dock that person a predetermined amount. Naturally, this requires some secretarial duty and minimal supervision on your part, but the results of a family working together will be worth your efforts.

Giving even small children daily household tasks is important because it's one way children learn to feel a part of the family. Don't worry if they're too young to complete the whole job. You can be helped by their doing just a part of the job.

One way to gain eager help from your young helpers is to give them important-sounding titles. The person in charge of cleaning bathrooms becomes "Washroom Attendant." Whoever is in charge of picking up living room clutter is the "Main Room Manager," and so on.

Of course, you want to avoid giving your children mindless chores without considering their interests and abilities. (And their abilities do change rapidly as they grow!) Imagine my surprise when I left the ironing board for just a few minutes and returned to find my daughter proudly displaying the garment she had very satisfactorily ironed. She had discovered a new skill that she obviously enjoyed, so I quickly took her off pickup duty and put her in charge of those 100 percent cottons that take so much time to iron.

Likewise, a teenage boy would be delighted to have actual responsibility for washing the car, changing the oil, and filling up the gas tank. And an older daughter shouldn't always get stuck with cleaning up the dinner dishes. Give her special responsibilities as well. She could, for instance, be asked to assist little sister in her school clothes shopping. The idea is to make some responsibilities an honor, so that children will be more likely to participate in family life.

But a word of caution. Since your children's abilities may exceed your wildest expectations, don't be tempted to overdo. Remember, even your teens are still your older *children*.

Be careful not to overburden them with chores. Special consideration should always be made for homework overloads, after-school activities and jobs, or just plain goofing off now and then. You'll recognize your family's happy medium by remembering that the quality of your children's lives should not suffer because you work, but rather be enhanced.

A Good Idea!

Set up a job chart for the family. List all the chores that have to be done. Divide the chart into those jobs which need to be done alone and those which require a team effort. Ask family members to sign up for the jobs they want.*

---

*The Home & School Institute, *Families Learning Together* (New York: Wallaby Books, 1980).

CLOSE TABS ON FAMILY RECORDS

When was the last time you couldn't find an important paper that you knew you had put away very carefully? A personal data system will put an end to such dilemmas and keep your home office organized besides!

If you don't have room for a small two-drawer filing cabinet, purchase accordion folders or a storage chest that fits under the bed or substitute with sturdy cardboard boxes of appropriate size.

Use the following checklist to remind yourself what to keep and what to discard.

Active File
Tax receipts
Paid bill receipts
Current canceled checks
Unpaid bills
Current bank statements
Income tax working papers
Health benefit information
Insurance policies
Family health records
Receipts of items under warranty
Receipts of items not yet paid for
Credit card information
Copies of wills
Appliance manuals and warranties
Education information
Loan payment books
Loan statements

Items to Discard
Salary statements

Other records no longer needed
Expired warranties
Coupons after expiration date

Safe Deposit Box
Birth certificates
Marriage certificates
Divorce decrees
Death certificates
Titles to automobiles
Veterans' papers
Contracts
Citizenship papers
Adoption papers
Wills
Deeds
Household inventory
Bonds and stock certificates

ESCAPING THE TELEPHONE TRAP
Many women are disorganized simply because they've fallen victim to telephone abuse. The telephone can absolutely wreck our daily living pattern if we don't place restrictions on its use in our life.

If friends call you from early in the morning until late at night, install an answering machine to free you from these untimely intrusions. When your chores are completed, you can then return the calls at your leisure. Other helpful hints:

1. Smile into the phone. When talking on the telephone, people have the tendency to mirror the personality of the other person.

So be friendly and offer a cheerful, wide-awake greeting. Speak clearly, listen attentively. And don't carry on a conversation with someone else (such as a child) near the phone.

2. If talking extends over a longer time than you'd like, here are some graceful ways to end a conversation:

"I know you're busy, so I'll let you go."

"Listen, I'm going to have to let you go."

"Can I call you back? I'm expecting a call."

"Can we continue this conversation sometime later? Maybe over lunch?"

But do use your judgment. There's nothing more painful than really needing to talk to someone, only to be told that the person "doesn't have time." We may have a million opportunities to minister on the telephone—let's be ready to truly make the most of them!

CHAPTER 5

Finding Private Time

All of us at some time or another relish the idea of getting away—as if moving the body to another location would be restful in itself. The irony of this thinking is that when we return, we face the same pressures and problems that we so eagerly left behind. True rest isn't in moving the body from one place to another. Nor is it in the absence of thinking.

The dictionary definition of "vacation" can give new insights to this often misinterpreted word. A vacation, says Webster, is time free for something else—specifically, time for contemplation. Certainly this is what most of us could use: time to discover ourselves, time to seek the kingdom of God, time for renewal. The marvelous thing about this kind of vacation is that we needn't have time off from our regular work schedule or a stashed away bundle of money in order to take advantage of it! I call such a vacation a *state-of-mind holiday.* Here are the rules of the game:

For two weeks, find vacation time for yourself in your everyday routine—one hour per day. Take on a particular project during this special hour, being careful not to exceed the allotted time period. Suggestions are given below, but follow your own instincts. You'll find a state-of-mind holiday both invigorating and stimulating.

"MIND" COLLECTING
What's required: A keen sense of observation; a reliable memory.
Benefits: The joy of being able to return to a scene many times.

Photography companies tell us to capture a moment on film, but there's really a much better way to cherish and keep the precious. I call this kind of savoring *"mind" collecting.* Its beauty lies in the fact that it doesn't require fancy equipment and is always available for the spontaneous joys of life. What better way to spend a vacation than taking mind pictures of a well-loved subject!

Choose any topic of interest—roses, chapels, trees, smiles, and so on. Then, for two weeks, implant these scenes or objects in your mind as you confront them. Record these "mind" scenes in a journal. You may be surprised to discover how much like poetry your descriptions will read.

HOME WORKSHOP
What's required: A spirit of creativity.
Benefits: Tangible rewards—completed projects.

Is there a hobby or pastime you never have time for these days? If so, the workshop holiday is a perfect solution, and one hour every evening or early morning for two weeks should enable you to get a pretty good start on a project—maybe even complete it! Go for simplicity—the small needlework piece instead of a large complicated one; the writing of fun limericks instead of deep, philosophical poetry. Four such vacations throughout the year could give you four handsome Christmas gifts for some very special people.

Is there something you'd like to learn? Studying isn't just for scholars. Become your own expert. Spend an hour every day for two weeks pursuing your special interest. Write a research paper on the topic. (Hand-bound and decorated copies would make interesting gifts.)

AROUND THE TOWN IN FOURTEEN DAYS

What's required: Untamed curiosity; an appreciation for the past and present.

Benefits: Greater knowledge of your local surroundings; civic pride.

This two-week vacation begins at work on your lunch break and is an interesting way to become acquainted with your community or do those things for which you've never made time.

Prepare for your journey by scanning city brochures and newspapers for places you've never been that are within reasonable distance of your office. Then make a list. Perhaps you'll eat lunch at that tiny Mexican café you've always wondered about. Maybe you'll visit a vintage clothing store and purchase something nostalgically romantic. Could be you'll walk to City Hall or rest your feet beside a "downtown" fountain. The key is to shed inhibitions and explore. And remember, whatever you select to do must be brand new!

When the weekend arrives, you can be generous and share this part of your vacation with the family. Go fishing at a forest preserve, do a little local sight-seeing, or visit the library and dig up local history.

FINDING UNITY WITH GOD
What's required: A love of God; a desire to be at one with him.
Benefits: A change of thought; a refreshed spirit.

Plan two weeks of simple menus with easy cleanup features such as paper plates. (Make certain your family knows it's only temporary.) This should give you an extra hour in the evening. While the children are playing or watching television, find yourself a quiet nook—preferably an area with a door you can close. Now delve into Bible study and prayer.

Choose a particular area of interest—forgiveness, temptation, grief. Check out special concordances and study aids from your church or public library; purchase a Bible study book; or keep a spiritual diary. The sense of calmness and inspiration that you discover during a spiritual vacation won't end with the closing of your books but will follow you throughout your resumption of routine chores.

A Menu of Mind Resters
Listen to records
Daydream for a specified time
Sit in a garden
Ride a horse
Sew a simple pattern
Work on your family photo album
Make a rag doll
Create a potpourri

PRECIOUS MOMENTS

There's no question that a state-of-mind holiday leaves one feeling renewed. But an occasional effort at finding time for yourself is not really enough to ensure a balanced life-style. Relaxing or thinking on a regular basis is an important human need. "Self-time" may even be one way of easing stress. This time is different from pleasant moments with family and friends—"self-time" is the setting aside of hours from both work and relationships.

Yet working mothers often claim such time is nonexistent, or at least not available on a regular basis.

"I've *tried* to set aside time for painting,"

said one woman, "but every time I manage a few moments to myself, the girls come up with an emergency for me to take care of."

As she spoke, her female listeners nodded in recognition of the problem. There are only so many hours in a day. But a closer look at our personal schedules will actually reveal all kinds of wonderful opportunities for private moments *within* our already hectic routine. We find such moments through proper utilization of "found" time, making better use of existing, untapped time. Sound impossible? Certain you haven't a spare second in your already too-crowded day? Look again. Though none of us will find it in exactly the same places, all of us can find some of this valuable time for rest and revitalization by simply using our imagination.

Get started today. Find your hidden moments of privacy by exploring a few of the following ideas—all tried and tested by busy women like you.

• Ride the bus instead of driving your own car to work. A friend told me, "It does take more time, but it's *my* time. I read the newspaper, work crossword puzzles, and sometimes even pray."

If public transportation to your job isn't available, you may be able to claim the same quiet time by joining a car pool.

• Take advantage of "waiting" time. Whether seated in the crowded waiting room of your doctor's office or in the plush reception area of a Fortune 500 company, you can collect valuable moments for personal use while waiting. Some things you can do in this situation are: prepare shopping lists, write letters to relatives, catch up on your reading of business periodicals, etc. A former boss of mine never left the house—not even for an evening with hubby—without a book under her arm or tucked into her purse.

"It makes me anxious to have to sit in the car while he fills the tank with gas or drops by the office for a quick check," she said. "But if I have something to read, sitting in the car by myself somehow becomes *my* time, and I love it!"

- Use lunch hour as a breather instead of a noisy social hour. Some ways to do this are:
  1. Close your office door, dim the lights, and kick off your shoes. Sit at your desk and practice deep breathing for twenty minutes.
  2. Walk to a nearby park and enjoy a picnic for one . . . or just walk around the block for a quick energy recharger.
  3. Spend forty minutes browsing in the public library—you can't beat it for a quiet, restful atmosphere.
  4. Go home for a change of scenery.
  5. Walk through a nearby art museum.
- Make the ride home work for you—not against you. Listen to soothing Christian or classical tapes on your car's tape player. (If you don't have a tape player but drive long distances each day, consider installing one as a form of mental health insurance.)

• Take two vacation days and enjoy a four-day weekend. Hire a baby-sitter and do what *you* want to do, such as:

1. Hunt for clothing bargains.
2. Share a long lunch with someone dear.
3. Check into a beauty spa for the "works."

• Take a half-day off and go home to rest. Actually lie down on your bed with a cool compress on your forehead. When five o'clock arrives, pick up the children from their child-care facility as usual.

• Make a Do Not Disturb sign for your bedroom door and teach your children to respect it. Set aside a part of your day when you won't be interrupted and place the sign on your doorknob during this time. Read your favorite magazines or get into a new novel.

• Allow your children to watch one or two early evening television shows. Make yourself a glass of herb tea and sit on the patio while dinner cooks.

• Lock yourself in the bathroom and take a really long bath. Listen to motivational tapes via a battery-run tape player, give yourself a facial, or paint your nails.

• Take a bike ride. If you need an excuse, let the supermarket be your destination.

• Relax for twenty minutes on a homemade slantboard. Place the far end of your ironing board on the fireplace hearth and recline upon it. The inverted position allows gravity to work for you. As blood is brought to the head, the extra nourishment and oxygen will leave you feeling rested and peaceful.

• Go for a walk in the rain. If temperature

Tired or Bored?

Sometimes we think we're tired when we're really just bored. Fatigue and a worn-out feeling are often caused by unproductive mental attitudes. Reflect on the personalities of people you like to be around. Chances are, they're individuals who take responsibility for making their lives interesting and worthwhile. Here are tips on putting the "zip" back into your life—or keeping it there.

- Make an effort to really listen to everyone you encounter during the day. Even if they don't have anything terribly interesting to say, your sincere interest in these people may make their day more meaningful. When you look at it that way, can you afford to do less?
- Act enthusiastic even when you aren't. Acting so will eventually lead to the real thing. Besides, it's contagious and helps get the job done.
- Keep learning—and not just within your job. Learn to do things which give you satisfaction away from your career identity—take up weaving, plant an herb garden, etc.
- Have something to look forward to each weekend. Plan on eating out Friday night, or take the children to the zoo on Saturday. It doesn't have to be anything elaborate—just a simple deviation from routine will recharge your energy and interest in life.

permits, don't cover up with rain gear. The rain will give your complexion a natural, healthy glow—you'll look as relaxed as you feel.

AVOIDING THE POST-VACATION BLUES

Have you ever returned from a wonderful vacation and suddenly been hit with a case of the blues? A vacation of the mind can leave you just as wilted as a real trip away from home if you don't prepare for coming back. Here are a few ideas that work well for returning after any kind of vacation.

1. Make certain your house is picked up before you retreat for your holiday. It will be much more pleasant to rejoin the family if chores are completed and your household is in order.

2. Make a list of things that must be done after the two-week vacation. Put it in a prominent place. Just having it there will take the worry out of not doing something you feel you should be doing.

3. Don't leave your holiday cold turkey. Pamper yourself for a few days afterward with dinner out after work, or perhaps with the purchase of a good novel.

Nutrition:
What's for Dinner?

It was dinnertime. Mary placed her briefcase on the kitchen counter and handed her husband the sack of hamburgers.

"I've got to change clothes," she greeted him apologetically.

Once in the bathroom, she slipped into jeans, splashed cool water on her face, and listened to the clamor of three preschoolers discovering the aroma of fresh hamburgers. How well she could visualize the scene—the tearing of papers, the grabbing for french fries, and the crying for ketchup.

But everyone likes hamburgers, Mary reasoned to herself. *We used to think they were treats when I was a kid.*

So why did she feel guilty? What was so wrong with dinner these days that she'd rather stay in the bathroom than join the family? Mary didn't really need an answer—she knew. This was the third hamburger meal she'd served her family over a ten-day span.

I must be the worst mother in the world,

she thought as a tear trickled down her face.

But she isn't—we all know that. Though three hamburgers in ten days may seem to be overdoing it a bit, we understand completely when it comes to tempting the palates of preschoolers and answering the need for dinner.

DINNERTIME BLUES

If there is one area of life in which American women suffer universal twinges of guilt, dinnertime would win hands down. Today's mother has the additional responsibility of teaching her children about exercise and proper nutrition. But how to do this at the end of a working day is another matter entirely.

Part of the problem may be that we set standards for dinner that are no longer applicable in today's world. It has, for instance, taken many years for me to accept the fact that after-work dinners can never compare to the evening meals I enjoyed as a child. Growing up as a missionary kid in pre-industrial Nigeria, I was accustomed to long, peaceful dinners of spectacular dishes served by white-coated servants. After dessert, my parents would rise from the table and take us children for a walk on the compound. When we returned, the table had been cleared, the dishes washed, and the tilly lantern lit. How can I live up to that?

I can't. Modern life calls for tasty, quickly prepared foods that can be eaten with a minimal amount of pomp and fuss. Consequently, I've given up the notion that dinner has to be a certain type of food served in a particular way. My present goal is simply to present the most nutritious meal possible in the most cheerful manner. On some days this might, indeed, be a hamburger from a fast-food restaurant; but on others it may be steamed vegetables and fresh fruits. The point is: As long as we are striving to feed our family with love *and* care, dinner can be a celebration of family life, no matter what the menu or environment.

PUTTING IT ON THE TABLE

Through the years I've found planning to be the key to happy, nutritious weeknight dinners. For me it all begins on Friday lunch hour when I make out the upcoming week's menus. I ask myself how many meals I need to plan for, and later that night I check foods on hand for leftover possibilities. Then I make a food list for shopping. During the week I've checked the newspaper for specials and clipped coupons for foods that we normally use.

Working mothers don't have a wide choice of shopping hours. We can go at the end of a work day and possibly spend more because we're tired and hungry, or we can go on the weekend. Saturday mornings are usually the least crowded of the weekend hours, and if your husband's home, you can even sneak away without little ones underfoot.

Hints for Making Dinner Easier on Mom

1. Stick to simple meals: chef salad, London broil, baked chicken, etc.
2. Learn to clean up as you cook. This will keep you from facing an overwhelming job later.
3. Give your husband a homemade cookbook of fool-proof recipes. Consider assigning cooking days between the two of you. (A teenager can also take a turn.)
4. Post weekly menus on the refrigerator door so the family will know what's for dinner and you're spared the annoying question as you walk in from work.
5. Keep an ongoing grocery list of items needed in a conspicuous spot where everyone may add on.
6. If energy permits, cook the night before. For instance, brown and cook a roast for one hour; refrigerate. Peel vegetables. Store in container in refrigerator. Next evening, combine ingredients and cook for another hour.
7. Cook double the amount needed. Arrange leftover portions in oven-proof or microwave dishes. Seal and freeze for future use.
8. Consider the benefits of investing in a microwave oven. Quick defrosting, retention of valuable nutrients, and fast meal preparation are considered well worth the cost for most working mothers.

Every working mother should keep a scrapbook or file box of easy-to-prepare, nutritious meals. If you haven't already begun such a collection, you'll find these recipes in magazines, cookbooks, and by word of mouth. Your criteria for judging such menus: ready availability of ingredients, easy preparation, healthy nutrition, and moderate-to-low calorie content. Sometimes the idea is common enough, but it's having it there in front of you that makes recall quicker and easier. Here are some family favorites to help you get started.*

English Muffin Pizza
Split and arrange on baking sheet:
6 English muffins
Combine in bowl:
2 cups tomato sauce
1 teaspoon salt
½ teaspoon pepper
½ teaspoon oregano
½ teaspoon Italian seasoning
¼ teaspoon garlic salt
Coat muffins with tomato mixture.
Sprinkle on:
2 cups grated cheese
Add:
pepper slices
pepperoni slices
mushrooms
Heat in 350° oven until cheese is bubbly.
Serve with green salad and brownies.

*Unless otherwise stated, recipes are suitable for serving a family of four.

Steamed Vegetables

Prepare any vegetable such as broccoli, cauliflower, turnips, or carrots by cooking in steamer until tender.

Stuffed Bell Peppers for Six

Prepare six peppers by slicing off top and removing seeds. Cook in small amount of water until tender. Drain and set aside.
Cook according to directions:
1 package of Rice-a-Roni Spanish Rice Mixture
Arrange cooked peppers in large baking dish. Spoon Spanish rice mixture into each pepper. Place extra rice in baking dish between peppers.
Sprinkle:
½ cup grated cheese on top
Bake in 350° oven for 15–20 minutes. Serve with pineapple salad and hot rolls.

Pork Chops Creole

4 pork chops ½–¾" thick
1 teaspoon salt
¼ teaspoon pepper
4 thin onion slices
4 tablespoons uncooked instant rice
1 8-oz. can stewed tomatoes
4 green pepper slices
In a 10-inch skillet, brown chops over medium heat. Sprinkle with salt and pepper. Top each chop with onion slice, pepper ring, 1 tablespoon rice, and 1/4 cup tomatoes. Reduce heat; cover and simmer until tender—about 45 minutes. (Add small amount of water during cooking if necessary.) Serve with

buttered green beans, cottage cheese, and peach salad. For dessert: ice cream and cookies.

Family Casserole
Cook according to package directions:
1 cup macaroni
Drain and add:
1 can chunk white chicken
1 can cream of chicken soup
Sprinkle top with 1 cup crushed potato chips. Bake in 350° oven for 30 minutes. Serve with green peas and biscuits.
For evening snack: popcorn.

Sunday or Company Dinner:
Chicken and Rice
1½ cups uncooked rice
1 or 2 uncooked, cut up chickens
1 stick melted butter or margarine
1 pkg. dry onion soup mix
1 can cream of chicken soup
3 cups water
Salt and pepper to taste
Place uncooked rice in bottom of large baking dish. Arrange chicken on top of rice. Salt and pepper chicken. Pour melted butter and cream of chicken soup over chicken and sprinkle onion soup mix over it. Add water. Cover and cook for 2 hours at 350°.
Serve with broccoli and molded applesauce cinnamon Jell-O salad.

Applesauce Cinnamon Jell-O Salad
Prepare large package of cherry Jell-O with 2 cups boiling water. Add 2 cups cinnamon-flavored applesauce. Stir until contents are

dissolved. Allow to set in refrigerator until firm (several hours or overnight). May be served as salad or dessert.

Garden Omelet

Sauté in butter or margarine:
1 diced tomato
1 diced onion
1 diced green bell pepper
Set aside.
Beat together 3 eggs per person plus 1 table-spoon water for each serving. Pour egg mixture into heated frying pan. Cook without stirring until egg mixture is hard around the edges. Lift edges and let mixture flow underneath until omelet is cooked.
Add:
vegetables
1 cup grated cheese
Fold omelet in half and allow cheese to melt. Slide onto warm plate. Serve with sliced cantaloupe and hot biscuits.
For dessert serve snack cookies. Simply spread graham crackers with your favorite canned icing.

Spaghetti with Zucchini and Green Beans

3 cups diced zucchini (about ¾ lb.)
1 9-oz. pkg. frozen green beans
1 cup diced onion
1 teaspoon salt
¼ teaspoon pepper
¼ cup oil
1 16-oz. can tomatoes
4 tablespoons grated parmesan cheese
½ teaspoon thyme

1 12-oz. pkg. spaghetti, cooked and drained
In large saucepan, sauté zucchini, beans, onion, salt, and pepper in oil for 15 minutes or
until onion is tender and zucchini and beans
are tender-crisp. Stir in tomatoes, 2 tablespoons parmesan cheese, and thyme. Cook
10 minutes. Toss with hot spaghetti and
sprinkle with remaining parmesan cheese.
Serve with french bread and fruit.

How Even a Working Mom Can Improve Her Family's Diet

1. Bake, boil, and broil your meats and poultry.
2. Remove skin on poultry to cut down on fat.
3. Steam or microwave your vegetables to preserve nutrients.
4. Serve whole wheat bread.
5. Use lowfat milk.
6. Trim fat off meat before cooking.
7. Try seasoning with spices and herbs instead of salt.
8. Eat raw fruits and vegetables whenever possible.

Quick and Easy Lunches to Pack or Eat at Home
Sandwiches
On a bagel: Tuna salad topped with cheese. Broil
until cheese melts.
On whole wheat bread: Egg salad, leftover meat-
loaf.
On french bread: Salami, provolone cheese, toma-
to, and onion.

On a hot dog bun: Canned chili and frankfurter.

Soup

Carry in an insulated container. Eat with crackers and thick slices of cheese. Take advantage of instant soups that are packaged in disposable cups.

Salad

Wash greens when you first bring them home from the grocery store. Place in an air-tight container, and you'll be ready to prepare your salad any time. Add tomatoes, cucumbers, onions, etc. Your favorite low-calorie dressing and cottage cheese complete the meal.

Hot Meal

Serve baked beans on brown bread toast with potato chips and pickles.

SHOULD YOU OR SHOULDN'T YOU?

During the early months of my new career, I was often frustrated when I arrived home late to find my husband sitting in his chair waiting for me to start supper. I mentioned this in conversation to our art director one day and was surprised at her simple solution to the problem.

"Haven't you learned about frozen pot pies?" she asked. "They may not be everyone's favorite, but when it's late and the family's hungry, why add to the disagreeable atmosphere by arguing over dinner preparations?"

I took the woman's advice to heart and have since made it a habit to keep some type of frozen dinner on hand at all times. And in truth, it works better if the entree *isn't* a family favorite because it's more likely to stay around for a true emergency.

On the other hand, frozen foods needn't be considered just an emergency food item. Though usually more expensive than canned goods, frozen foods keep longer than fresh foods and are a great deal faster to cook in many cases.

Tips on Purchasing Frozen Foods

1. Pick up frozen foods on your way to the check-out counter.
2. Buy only clean, undamaged packages. Report soggy, limp packages to the store's manager.
3. Avoid heavily frosted boxes—they may have been defrosted and refrozen.
4. Make certain that all frozen foods are packed together. Not only do they stay cooler that way, but it will be easier for you to put them quickly away once you are home.
5. In very hot weather, you may find that placing frozen foods in an insulated bag or an ice chest with a thin layer of ice on the bottom will help them arrive home with your food in more stable condition.

SWEET TALK

All well-informed mothers know the merits of nutritious goodies versus empty calories. Perhaps the real issue is whether or not we practice what we know.

So don't resort to expensive sugar-coated

snacks. Healthy, nutritious snacks will not only give your child (or husband) more energy, but save you money as well.

Here are some kid-tested snack ideas:

- Fresh fruits and vegetables. Skewer fruit or vegetable pieces on a toothpick for mini-kabobs, dip in orange juice, and roll in chopped peanuts. Stuff celery with tuna salad, cream cheese, peanut butter, or cottage cheese.
- Popcorn. Homemade, if you please. And without butter and salt!
- Whole grain crackers spread with herb-seasoned cottage cheese mixed with plain yogurt and grated carrots.
- Pocket salad sandwiches—pocket bread stuffed with mixed vegetable salad. (A spoon of salad dressing is optional.)
- A large dill pickle wrapped in a slice of American cheese.

CHAPTER

7

Special Family Times

Can you remember:
 My Weekly Reader
 Dodge ball
 Roy Rogers
 Recess
 Coke floats
 Spaghetti-strapped sundresses?

So can I. I also remember making jelly tarts
out of Mother's dough scraps and playing
tiddly-winks on the floor with Daddy. Which
brings to mind the question: What will my
child remember twenty years from now—
day school and yogurt pops? Perhaps.

But there is another possibility. What if we
pull together and create real homes with loving and caring at the center of the hearth?
Instead of wishing our children "a good day"
as they leave for school or another activity,
why not strive to see that they do indeed
have a good day? Why not *give* them a good
day they will remember for years to come?

Take note that I am not talking about striving to give a material blessing in this instance, but rather seeking to share what will result in an improved mental and spiritual state. Giving in this way is highly enriching to the benefactor as well as the recipient.

MAKING CONTACT

A busy journalist discovered how to give her three children the gift of a continued sense of good things to come by preparing personalized gift certificates. Propped up in bed one night, she made a list of all of her children's favorite things that she seldom had time to supervise—a pizza picnic, blueberry muffins, charades and popcorn, etc. Then, using ordinary index cards and colored pens, she wrote out certificates for each child. One child received a certificate for a visit to the fire station, another received a certificate to go to a high-school basketball game, and the third received a certificate worth sixty minutes of playing kickball with Mother.

You don't have to make certificates for special moments, but the system may help commit you to some of the larger projects. Smaller activities can be spontaneous— though you may want to consult your list every now and then. Here are a few ideas for Mom or Dad to build from.

1. Look at clouds
2. Snap fresh beans
3. Watch the sunrise
4. Fly a kite
5. Make ice cream

6. Jump in a pile of leaves
7. Drink a cup of cocoa
8. Eat by candlelight
9. Play a board game
10. Go horseback riding
11. Hold hands
12. Take the stairs instead of an elevator
13. Take the elevator instead of the escalator
14. Take a hike
15. Build a fire
16. Go roller skating
17. Clean out a closet
18. Pop popcorn
19. Barbecue
20. Dance crazy dances
21. Make muffins
22. Make a picture book
23. Write to the President
24. Start a leaf collection
25. Go from morning until lunch using only one hand
26. Draw a map of the community
27. Collect and press wild flowers
28. Roast marshmallows on an open fire

Another important point of contact to make with your child is to let him see you in your office environment. Make arrangements with your boss to bring him in for half a day. (Christmas may be a good time to do this because everyone's feeling kind and benevolent and usually work schedules aren't as tight.) Since your child should be old enough not to disturb others when you attempt this activity, you can give him a new coloring book and crayons or some quiet game suited to his age and let him entertain himself as you go about your work.

EVENTS FOR EVERYONE

There are other fun activities that belong to everyone—both children and parents. These special family activities require the cooperation and enthusiasm of each family member for true success.

Post news of upcoming family times on a bulletin board or refrigerator. Your children will soon be watching this "information center" with excited anticipation.

Of course, there is always the obvious—a picnic, a community play, the circus. Don't underestimate the fun behind ordinary events. (I can still remember the thrill of *every* picnic we went on when I was a child.) Besides, you can always add a surprise angle. For instance, one woman packed individual box suppers for her family in decorated gift boxes. Another idea is to have an indoor picnic on a dreary, rainy day. Be as "corny" as you like—it's one of the privileges of belonging to a family.

Other ideas:

• Introduce a family game night. Play *Clue, Monopoly, Scrabble,* and so on. Serve Coke floats for a special snack.

• Take a ball to the nearest swimming pool and play catch.

• Create comics with a message. Cut comic strips from the daily or Sunday newspaper. White out the dialogue with Liquid Paper.

Have your family change the story to demonstrate Christ's love for us.

• Give each family member the opportunity to tell a joke at the dinner table.

• Schedule a checkers championship. Each family member plays one game with every other family member. Keep track of the winners. The person with the best win-loss record is the champ.

• Build a family collage. It should contain small objects that have had emotional meaning for each member of the family during the year. Programs, school papers, tickets, etc., are good items to start with.

• Create a housemark or family monogram using the family name. Example: Combine the last name plus the first initial of each family member. The housemark is selected by the whole family. From there, encourage family members to stencil the design onto personal property. Dad or an older child could even carve the housemark above a door frame.

• Begin a family journal. Purchase an attractive "blank" book and explain to the family that everyone is invited to contribute to its contents. Place it in a visible spot along with a pen. Descriptions of great family moments, news clippings, poetry, and personal insights on family situations are all viable contributions.

• Build a family vegetable garden. Allow each family member to be in charge of one vegetable of his choice.

• Have a "treat the family like company"

night. Prepare a special dinner, set the table with your best dishes, candles, and a centerpiece. Naturally, everyone comes to the table not necessarily dressed up, but at least pleasantly groomed.

• Plan a "do something nice for someone else" night. As a family unit, select someone who could use some cheering up. It could be a shut-in church member, a new child on the block, or a special relative who's down and out. Now let each family member decide what he can give. Though everyone's abilities will be different, here are a few suggestions.

1. Write a poem.
2. Paint a picture.
3. Sing a song.
4. Tell a funny story.
5. Make a flower arrangement.
6. Bake cookies.
7. Write a letter.

• Give a grocery party. Everyone in the family gets to select one item at the grocery store (unbeknown to each other) for a meal. The surprising mix can make for a hilarious, fun-filled evening.

• Designate a family worship hour. If you can't realistically gather more than once a week, do so then! Something is better than nothing. Sing songs, follow a family devotional guide, and pray sentence prayers. During the rest of the week, remember to pray at mealtimes and to share in bedtime communication with God.

And the list of things to do with your family could go on and on and on. . . . Why not pledge to stop and smell the roses with your family today? As you do, remember to save some time for just being there and telling each child how much you love and appreciate him.

Finding Time to Care

Women are busier these days—most of us really don't have as much time to attend to the needs of others as our mothers did. And yet people in our communities and extended families are still giving birth, still dying, still undergoing operations, and being part of all the other events of life that call for care-giving. So when our mothers can no longer do the giving, who's going to take over? Here are practical ways busy women can help, too:

1. Offer to pick up some books for the recuperating person—or bring some of your own.

2. Pay for a one-time housecleaning job or help the person in need by checking into available social services. Ill or elderly people often don't have the strength or know-how to get such services started.

3. Record church services for those who aren't able to attend.

4. Carry a single rose to a shut-in.

5. Send cards to the sick—daily. Call for a brief chat when you're sure they're feeling well enough.

6. Take a loaf of fresh french bread and a pound of butter to someone who needs a lift.

7. Instead of flowers, consider giving the hospitalized patient an especially pretty pillowcase. It will pick up spirits by bringing a homelike atmosphere into the hospital room.

8. Remember the family during times of crisis. Perhaps your greatest gift could be giving someone an hour off from bedside sitting.
9. Upon a death in a family, take them a can of coffee, eggs, and muffins instead of the customary casserole.
10. Look for ways of doubling up when friends or family need attention. A big stew, for instance, could feed another family as well as yours. A trip to the zoo could include the child of a sick mom. One woman does laundry for friends who need help. Or you might do shopping or run errands for someone else while you do your own.
11. Take a complete meal to a family in need by utilizing the following recipe. (Multiply amount by number of persons being served.)
    Wash and slice thinly:
    1 potato
    1 carrot
    1 onion
    ¼ green pepper
    small handful of fresh or frozen green beans
    Add:
    several chunks of cheese
    salt and pepper
    Wrap in:
    2 cabbage leaves
    Wrap all ingredients in aluminum foil. Place on cookie sheet and bake 30-35 minutes at 375°.

Discipline and Your Child

Heather has spent a lot of time on the bench during recess these past few years. It's her school's most formidable punishment for talking in class, being tardy, and so forth. Part of me doesn't mind that my active child is being reprimanded for her gregarious behavior—I was always so shy, I can't remember ever getting into trouble at school. But, on the other hand, some things are a mother's duty, and upholding school policy is one of them.

"Heather," I say, approaching the subject carefully, "were you the only one who had to sit on the bench?"

"Oh no," Heather answers, "everyone had to."

"Everyone?"

"Yeah," Heather answers, "everyone except the ones who didn't have to."

Dealing with bad behavior away from home is no easy feat for parents who weren't there when the supposed improper conduct took place. In all honesty, it's often hard to picture our children doing some of the things that are reported to us. Still, we usually feel we at least ought to try to mold their conduct outside of the home into an acceptable expression, even if we aren't there to see the results. And, of course, this has to be done in some way that doesn't impend on the child's sense of self-respect or his feelings about life.

Serious behavior problems call for outside counseling. But if it's ordinary, everyday behavior patterns that we're dealing with, parents can do more to improve the situation than anyone else.

DISCIPLINARY TACTICS

I come from a family that believed in directness. With my parents there was never a question as to how we kids were to behave when away from home—they told us. Furthermore, I've found this system works just as well today as it did back then. Try it.

When you receive a report of poor conduct, simply appeal directly to your child. Tell him how you feel and ask that the behavior be stopped. Explain why such behavior is inappropriate, but be ready to show affection. You'll find this approach suitable for all ages and just about any behavior situation. As an added plus, you'll probably be pleasantly surprised at how easy it is.

If this tactic doesn't work, you can always go the incentive route. Promises of future pleasure can be used to start and stop behavior patterns. One year when I was having a particularly hard time getting the point across, my husband and I awarded Heather gold stars for each day of good school conduct. Heather wanted a pair of roller skates, so we decided a hundred stars would earn the skates. It took months. But in the slow process of earning those skates, our daughter mastered self-control in classroom talking.

An older child may be more interested in working toward a certain privilege such as giving a party or being allowed to take on an outside job. And, no, this is not bribery. Look around you at today's premiums, sales incentives, and paychecks—all of life is made up of rewards for jobs well done.

When judging a child's behavior, however, always be sure to look at intent. Very often, what is misconstrued as bad behavior is only the child's inability to cope with a situation. This can be particularly true at school where some children may sincerely need parental help in developing good citizenship habits.

Consider the child who doesn't know how to whisper—no wonder he's always being called down. In this instance, why not instigate a whisper day and encourage your child with a game of all-day whisper practice on the weekend? Likewise, if aggressive action seems to be prominent school behavior, make a point of helping your child learn to express himself verbally. Help him see that he doesn't have to lose his position as a leader just because he's going to be acting in a less forceful manner.

As in other discipline areas, hunt for good days on which to praise your child and ignore a few of the "bad" reports. Our goal in promoting good classroom conduct is not only to help the teachers maintain an atmosphere conducive to learning, but to aid our children in becoming healthy, whole adults who can function in society at large.

But if classroom behavior problems seem easily solved—don't sit back and relax yet! Your expectations of good behavior should carry over into after-school care, summer camp, visits to friends' homes, etc.

HOW PERMISSIVE SHOULD I BE?

It has been said that part of disciplining is knowing what you expect from your children and being comfortable with those expectations. The problem is that today's parents aren't too sure where freedom to grow ends and permissiveness begins. Child care expert Dr. Benjamin Spock says parents can raise a child well even if they are too strict or too easy-going. According to him, the trouble occurs when we're strict out of hostility toward the child or permissive out of guilt.

The guilt factor is big among working mothers. For us, permissiveness may seem easier. We may let reports of bad behavior slip by because we feel that, had we been home, behavior problems would never have occurred. Or perhaps we learn about the problem at the end of a long day and simply don't have the energy to grab the bull by the horns.

When one mother received news from her

son's summer camp that he was wrecking the efforts of his counselor, she was defensive.

"Since he can't stay home during the summer, the least I can do is be understanding," she said.

But in truth, her kindness was doing more harm than good.

Dr. Lee Salk, professor of psychology and pediatrics at New York Hospital-Cornell Medical Center, said in a recent newspaper article that "permissiveness means no rules and regulations. But that's not caring," he said. "Children do not enjoy it, nor do they want a parent who sets no rules or standards of behavior."

THE RESPECT RULE

So children of all ages need behavior guidelines—even when we're not there to remind them. But what kind of rules should we set, and how do we enforce them when we're away from the scene?

Try beginning with just one rule, but insist that it be upheld. Call this rule *respect*. Respect for parents, respect for peers, respect for institutions, and respect for others' property. Here's how the rule works.

Respect for parents. Dolores Curran, author of *Traits of a Healthy Family*, says parents model respect within the family, and that if parents don't insist upon it for themselves, teachers, ministers, policemen, and other authority figures certainly won't receive it either. How right she is!

76

Respect may mean different things in different families, but in my family it means:

1. Children may not talk back to parents—though heated discussions are permissible.
2. Children may not use language that parents do not approve of or use themselves.
3. Children must ask permission before going to someone's house—even if it's only across the street; and they must telephone to ask to stay longer should that situation arise.

In return:

1. Parents must respect differing opinions.
2. Parents must speak politely to children.
3. Parents must avoid belittling remarks or highlighting the faults of children.
4. When leaving the house, parents should tell children where they are going, even if it's a quick, "I'm off to work now," and should telephone to say they'll be late.

Respect for peers. It's easy to see the interaction of respect between parents and children. The same principle works outside of the home as well. When we encourage our children to treat friends with the same kindness and respect Mom and Dad expect, they'll find themselves in appreciative company. Children who are required to be sensitive to the feelings of family members will naturally do so outside of the family. They will wait their turn, refrain from bullying, and help out when someone younger or weaker is in a bind.

Respect for institutions. When parents are strong institutional supporters, whether of school, day care, church, or camp, children sense it's not wise to buck the system. Why have Mom *and* the teacher on your case? But at the same time, children need to be secure in the knowledge that if things do go wrong, Mom and Dad won't defend an institution over a child without being absolutely certain of the true situation.

Respect for others' property. From their very early years, children should be taught to handle their friends' toys with the same care they do their own. As they grow older, however, disrespect for others' property can mean anything from writing on desks to stealing candy from the corner store. Whenever a child does show such lack of respect, he will grow only through *acceptance* of consequences. Perhaps you'll insist he wash down the desk or return the candy. Of such painful experiences great people are made.

By now you've probably discovered that helping children behave on their own two feet while away from home requires a lot of time and attention from us when they *are* home. Be patient if it seems to take an inordinate amount of time to get the point across. Remember how often you had to remind your toddler to say "thank you" before it became automatic? In matters of discipline, learn to give of yourself in a loving, caring manner, knowing that as you do so, you're helping your child develop the necessary self-discipline for maturity.

CHAPTER 9

Enjoying Marriage

During medical school, student marriages followed the law of the jungle—only the fittest survived. Every fall, the auxiliary newsletter contained a small box with this ominous notice: "Due to unusual circumstances, the following offices need to be refilled." The reality of divorce was accepted early on; some couples would make it all the way through school, others would not.

So we learned to be sophisticated and not show surprise at the latest divorce news. After all, not everyone wants to be married to a doctor anyway. But for those of us who did—and wanted to stay married to our particular doctor—the challenge was almost overwhelming.

Today I don't think any of us survivors would stand up and smugly give advice on how to stay happily married. We still live in such fragile glass houses ourselves. And yet, because a woman's personal growth inevitably has some effect upon her marriage, I felt it important to address this subject by highlighting the knowns in my own marriage. Obviously, I can't make guarantees on my marriage or yours. But what I can do is share a few of the things that have worked for Olie and me and some of the things that have not.

WHAT WORKS FOR US

I believe there are basically two factors necessary for a successful marriage. First, we have to acknowledge that marriage is the union of two independent beings who bring their individuality to the altar as a means of enriching the union. Though you've heard it a thousand times before, I would caution you against trying to remake your spouse or yourself. To blend into one is to invite the very dangerous ingredient of boredom into your lives.

Second, it's important to realize that a marriage has to be developed—not just in the early years, but for its duration. We can never afford the luxury of not working at our marriage.

People usually accept both of these facts readily enough but, unfortunately, do very little about them. So that you don't have to fall into the latter group, here are a few hints to aid you in the nourishment of your marriage.

1. Do the unpredictable now and then—the things you may want to do but that don't fit in with other people's perception of you. Dance the flame dance after dinner, serve a cheese tray instead of a meal, take flying

lessons, or wear outrageous costume jewelry.

As Olie and I journeyed out of our twenties, we noticed a curious thing. Our marriage was revitalized as each of us rediscovered our old selves. Talents and hobbies that had been shelved for years suddenly reappeared and we were more like the Olie and Jayne of our dating years than the Olie and Jayne of early marriage.

In a recent newspaper article, clinical social worker Gay Jurgens gave boredom as a major cause of divorce. She said that in the case of a dual-career marriage, home often becomes little more than a resting place. When a couple's entire energy is turned to separate careers, there's simply none left for the development of the marriage.

So really work on being an interesting person full of surprises. Keep the brain stimulated with learning, accept life's challenges, and experiment with the "new." Forget about your job and take a camping trip or join forces with your husband on a community project. You'll be surprised at how even small things can give you more to talk about and make you feel closer.

2. Be responsible for your own state of happiness, then share it joyously with your spouse. Keep in mind that it isn't your spouse's responsibility to make you happy. Get out and find friends, hobbies, or a job that will make you happy.

During especially low points in our lives, Olie and I have a tendency to lean heavily on each other for personal happiness. It almost never works. It usually isn't until we seek out those things that make us whole as individuals that life begins to fall into place.

3. Tune into your spouse's concerns. True soul mates share each other's goals and aspirations. Some of these goals deserve joint efforts, while others need only your sincere and enthusiastic interest.

Getting through medical school was a joint project for Olie and me. But Olie's listening to my continuous monologue on writing projects was vital proof of his interest in me and was just as important as my helping to pay the bills.

Periodically, working couples need to examine their life together to discover if they're truly satisfied. Dissatisfaction can then be worked out by compromising or making a life-style change.

Invariably, success comes for one partner while the other is still "waiting." It's not easy to rejoice and be happy for your spouse in such instances—but it's absolutely imperative that you try! Celebrate each victory with dinner out, a cake from the bakery, or a congratulatory note. Attend each other's company parties. Make an effort to memorize names and faces of your spouse's fellow employees. Be willing to promote his work with any special skills you may have or by entertaining the boss. Ask questions about his work. Learn to share the exciting and meaningful aspects of yours—don't just bring home the problems. When couples are genuinely interested in each other's careers, loss of interest in the marriage is less likely to happen.

The road may be more difficult if you're married to a superachiever, however. Mary Alice Kellogg, author of *Fast Track*, says such people are often self-centered, and it's important to realize *you* won't get the nurturing you may desire from such a mate. A superachiever is rarely home.

And *his* job always comes first. It can be very discouraging to have to pack up and leave your good job to follow this man around the country. But if this is your problem, be patient and wait upon the Lord. Let your career take a backseat for now. A part-time job in your field or the pursuit of an advanced degree will keep your knowledge and skills updated. In the meantime, do have a life of your own. Those married to superachievers need to develop a strong self-identity and be able to enjoy living—even in their husband's absence.

4. Treat your spouse with the same tenderness you showed during courtship. Here are some specific ideas:
   a. Listen to him carefully.
   b. Say thank you.
   c. Make something special for him—a sweater, a cake, etc.
   d. Send him flowers.
   e. Touch him often, but never hang on him.

f. Play a special song on the jukebox for him.
g. a favorite candy bar in his briefcase.
h. When sending him off on a business trip, pack your picture and one of the children in the middle of his suitcase.
i. Mail a card to his office.
j. Greet him at the end of the day with a hug.

SPECIAL POINTERS

• Always resolve your differences before retiring for the night. Sometimes after an argument, people wake up determined to put yesterday behind them. But it's probably more common for unresolved arguments to quietly smolder until the next big flare-up.

• Make appointments with each other. A "date" per week is not a luxury but an essential element for a healthy, happy marriage. If finances are tight and the cost of a babysitter is prohibitive, talk with other mothers about forming a Friday night baby-sitting co-op.

• Don't spend all your weekend time catching up on chores. Take Saturday or Sunday afternoon off to go to the lake or country. When you must tackle housecleaning, be clear about the division of chores, perhaps using a written contract.

• Rather than waste time arguing or pouting, decide together what kind of activities you will or will not participate in on your time off. The same can be said about which people you will or won't spend time with. Be careful not to schedule every minute—allow for free time so you won't always be in a hurry.

• Telephone each other for a brief chat during the work day. Jog together in the evening. Stay up late one night a week.

• Things that don't work for us:
  1. Nagging about faults
  2. Keeping secrets
  3. Interrupting

CONDITIONS TO BE AVOIDED

Certain conditions really do seem harmful to sound marriages, but you can control many of these factors so that your marriage environment is a healthy one. Unhealthy conditions that you can control are:

• Lack of privacy. This can occur when children are allowed to stay up too late in the evenings.

• Noise pollution. There is always background noise coming from either the television or radio.

• Poor self-image. One or both spouses suffer from lack of self-respect.

Most of all, it's important to remember that people who have good marriages aren't any smarter, better, or luckier than those who don't. Those of us who have been married long enough to beat the national odds may give the impression of leading perfect lives and having it all together, but we don't.

We, too, have problems with money, boredom, jealousy, and the like. But we believe in marriage to the extent that we work these problems out within the marriage. In this respect, I hope all of us who are happily married will lend support to other married couples. People need to be reassured that in spite of the world's message, divorce isn't the only way to improve one's situation.

With a lot of work and perseverance, we can find ourselves, enjoy happiness, and know true freedom—all within the bounds of matrimony.

Self-Employment: When Home Is Where the Office Is

by Ruth Senter

I have been a mother for eighteen years. Nineteen years ago I published my first magazine article. Five books and hundreds of articles later, I am still getting my family happily involved in work, play, or school, putting the breakfast dishes in the dishwasher, sweeping the crumbs from the kitchen floor, climbing the stairs to my office, and sitting down to my word processor for a busy day of work. No rush hour traffic to fight or snow to scrape from my car windows. No splashing through puddles in the parking lot or waits at the coffee machine. I go to work without a coat and never have to worry about forgetting my umbrella.

Despite the apparent advantages of being self-employed and working out of my home, not all has been easy street. In fact, watching the crabapple blossom just outside my office window and hearing the birds chirp at the feeder below are small compensations when it comes to figuring out self-employment taxes, convincing the PTA committee that, in fact, I do work and am not available at 10:00 A.M. every third Thursday, or planning the monthly budget when I don't know when article payments will arrive. Earning money and staying home to do it are not an easy mix. Fortunately, with determination, discipline, and a strong, resonant, "I'm sorry I'm working that day," it can be done.

YOUR IDENTITY AS A WORKING MOM

The place to start is to learn to think of yourself as a working mother. You are. Place is not that significant. What you do with your time is.

I try to spend four days a week, nine to four, at my word processor. I am a writer. For me, writing is not a hobby, a fill-in, a leisure time activity. It is a paid profession. To make it pay, I must stick to regular work hours, say no to distractions, and learn to ignore the fingerprints I see on the wall as I start up the stairs to work. I must resist the urge to quickly throw in a load of laundry. I cannot afford to do it just because my office happens to be conveniently close to the washer and dryer.

If I take work seriously, I must learn to be emphatic with neighbors, friends, and family about my work schedule. They will think of me as I think of myself. If I think I should always be available and find it hard to tell them I'm not, my minutes will slowly get eaten up by coffee time at a neighbor's, school delivery of a forgotten English paper, or rummage sales for the PTA. I am not automatically available simply because I work at home. Others, especially family, must be reminded from time to time.

WHAT ABOUT PRESCHOOLERS?

Simple thing, you say, to make your fourteen year old understand why you cannot be interrupted by a forgotten term paper. But what about your three year old who has to know about the funny noise in the furnace—and he has to know it right now. Working at home when you have preschoolers hiding out under your desk or racing their Matchbox trucks over your manuscript pages is not so easily dealt with.

When my children were small, I promised myself I would work on my time, not their's. Admittedly, in those days, work at my desk was part time or less, but I was amazed at how quickly the bits and pieces of my day added up to valuable working time. The secret was to look for time fragments and immediately cash in on them: nap time, an hour here and there when my four year old was invited to play at the neighbor's, Saturday mornings when Daddy took the children to MacDonald's for breakfast. Instead of washing and waxing the kitchen floor when the children were not around, I went to my typewriter. In those days my floors didn't get waxed very often, but it was a small sacrifice for my commitment to my work.

In those days I also lived with greatly diminished expectations. I planned my days with plenty of time for interruptions. If I didn't expect to knock off two chapters in a day, I wasn't disappointed when the children came down with the croup and needed to be held or wanted to play Candyland for two hours of my morning. If, on the other hand, the day happened to hum along in precise peace and order and I got two chapters done because the kids entertained each other all day, it was a happy surprise—a bonus.

Reducing my "work-to-be-done" list meant that the children and I didn't end up resenting each other. I didn't resent them for fouling up my work expectations, and they didn't resent me for clicking the typewriter keys when they wanted me to move little red gingerbread boys around a board with them.

On the other hand, preschool days were still work days. When the children were old enough to understand, I did not hesitate to let them know that Mommy had a job she did at home. I managed to complete a master's in journalism and write two books during preschool days. True, my house was not immaculate and I didn't drink a lot of coffee with friends in those days, but by utilizing the time fragments I did have available, work was accomplished.

CREATING—AND KEEPING—
WORK SPACE

Working out of home also means distinguishing between the space called home and the space called work. I had to program myself to think of certain parts of the house as work space, even when my first office was in the laundry room next to the furnace. It did not look like an office with its tiny pine desk, which was a gift from my parents when I graduated from seventh grade, and two cardboard filing drawers. But calling it an office in my mind made me think *work* whenever I went near the laundry room.

Now that I have the luxury of an office, I make sure it looks more like an office than the guest bedroom it sometimes is. A large desk, plenty of drawer space, book shelves, and files have created an atmosphere conducive to work and efficient for organization.

I have also learned not to use my work space for home business. I do not phone the plumber or the dentist from my desk. Home business is conducted on the kitchen phone during nonwork hours. I keep the family calendar by the downstairs phone. Business appointments and schedules are made and kept for my office.

It is also easier to think *work* when I dress appropriately. I do not wear my jogging suit on days I am working in my office. Jogging suits are for the Saturday afternoon basketball games in front of the TV, not for work. I dress up to walk upstairs to my office—not always in silk blouses and gray suits, but in something that makes me feel more professional. I carry my purse with me into my office, not only because it is where I keep my glasses and my Day Timer organizer, but also to remind me that I'm going to work.

EXPECT TO JUGGLE MULTIPLE ROLES

Working out of my home means I have had to think of myself as part-time office secretary and janitor. I organize my work space and file papers every afternoon just before I quit for the day, and every morning before I begin work I empty my waste can. I also keep a list of supplies needed and every week I make a trip to the office supply store to replenish paper clips, file folders, or mailing labels. My trip to the office supply store also includes any xeroxing I need to do. Office supply stores often have xerox machines and are usually cheaper than the library, grocery store, or drugstore.

Since I am my own secretary, I must think *correspondence.* One morning a week I answer the week's mail. Keeping records is also up to me. A simple financial record book has made life much easier—a page for "Office Supply Expenses," one for "Work Submitted: Date, To Whom, Payment Received," and a third for "Mileage and Travel Expenses." My little black record book is vital toward tax time when I turn over my records to our accountant. It makes it easier to estimate earnings for paying the estimated income tax which is a part of life for the self-employed.

WORKING ALONE:
HOW TO COMPENSATE

There is a lonely side to working out of your home—no movement of bodies through the hall, no lunchroom chatter or frivolity around the coffee machine. While an absence of other people can have a down side, I work hard to fill my life with people at other times. Often I meet a friend for lunch, just like I would do if I had an office outside my home. Sometimes I invite a friend who has the same work schedule I do to come and eat her brown-bag lunch with me. She needs to be back in her office by one o'clock and so do I. We both understand commitment to work schedules.

When possible, I allow one day a week for home business—grocery shopping, cleaning, dentist and doctor's appointments, coffee with a friend, luncheons for church or school. Sometimes when fun activities, like the spring luncheon at high school, come on a work day, I treat myself to the luncheon and make up the three hours on Friday when I usually take care of home matters. I find I am more content working at home without people if I find nonworking hours to be with them.

I also compensate for the aloneness of the job by squeezing into my day some of my favorite things, like a fifteen-minute walk to the deli for a cup of coffee at ten in the morning or a quick stop by the bakery for a cinnamon roll on the way home from driving the children's car pool. Little favors to myself are important trade-offs for not being surrounded by people in my work.

"Does your mommy work?" I overheard a little friend ask my daughter Jori one day when she was small. "Oh, she doesn't work . . . she just types," was her candid reply. I laughed to myself. Such are the fantasies about the mother who works at home. "She doesn't work . . . she just types."

But when all is said and done, despite the fantasies, life for the woman who conducts business out of home can be rewarding and fulfilling. If only she learns to say to the PTA committee, "I'm sorry, I'm not available. I have to work that day. . . ."

A Business of Your Own?

Leaflets on various aspects of home businesses are available free of charge from the Small Business Administration. A list of titles may be obtained by writing the SBA at P.O. Box 15434, Fort Worth, TX 76119. A booklet entitled "Starting and Managing Your Own Business from Your Home" is available for $1.75 from the Consumer Information Center, Department 146R, Pueblo, CO 81009.

Five Questions from Working Mothers

Someone at work is always having a baby or celebrating some other type of milestone that calls for baked goods or a lunchtime casserole. What do I do— run myself ragged after work filling orders, or ignore the pleas for help and look unfriendly?

You don't have to do either. Your choices are: (1) Stop by the bakery and purchase the goods; or, (2) Select simple recipes that call for very little cooking and cleanup.

If you opt for the first choice, you can easily replace the bakery's white box with your own plate and plastic wrap. Though you have nothing to hide, your own plate will attract less attention and probably make you feel more comfortable. Another approach is simply to serve the food in its bakery container with no apologies or remorse about not having time to cook. After all, you're a working woman. Your first priority when on the job is getting the work done—not entertaining other office employees.

As for casseroles, you can solve this problem easily enough by becoming known as the dessert lady. Tell the party's organizer that you're happy to help with dessert, but simply can't manage a main dish. In no time at all, people will be enthusiastically asking you to make your "house" specialty.

My son's school is forever asking parents to work in carnival booths, collect newspapers, bake cakes, or cook hamburgers for various fund-raising drives. I don't want to appear uninterested— for both my son's and the school's sake. But since I don't have time for these activities, I find myself resenting them. Is there a good way to say no?

Schools often make a working mother feel less than adequate with their numerous requests for parental involvement. Working mothers can't sew costumes, take part in telephone chains, and bake cakes like their nonworking sisters. But there are other options. The next time you feel pressed to offer your help, consider the many business-related services you might be able to offer. Free printing, a supply of envelopes, samples, or even a financial lead should make a lot more sense than struggling with the contribution of a cake. Just don't give away anything that's not within your jurisdiction to do so!

Our child's teacher invariably schedules conferences during peak work

hours. Not only is it embarrassing to ask off, it's highly frowned upon in my company. How can I get the teacher to be more sensitive toward my situation?

School conferences are a dilemma for both teachers and mothers. Keep in mind that the teacher doesn't want to work after hours either! The easiest solution is for both parents to alternate taking off for these conferences. But another approach is to face the issue head-on: Write a note to your child's teacher explaining that while you are interested in your child's progress, a conference scheduled during work hours means loss of income for you or loss of respect from your boss—neither one satisfactory. Ask if the conference couldn't be scheduled before 8:00 A.M. or as close to 5:00 P.M. as possible. As a last resort, consider arranging a telephone conference after work. Do carry on such a conversation in your bedroom with the door shut, so that you will have the same privacy you would encounter in a school conference.

My friends are some of my most valuable resources, yet now that I'm working, I find them slipping away one by one. How can I find time for these people who mean so much to me?

It's wise to recognize the importance of friendship in a working woman's life. Friends not only support and add balance to our lives, they are very often God's instruments to help us grow.

At first glance it may seem you have merely traded friends from one area of your life for the people you work with. But look carefully. Work relationships can be superficial, and acquaintances are not necessarily friends. Besides a husband to talk to, we still need a good woman friend whom we can confide in and trust. But to keep in touch with such a person requires a sincere desire and effort on both people's part. And because one person will have to make the first move, it might as well be you.

Begin by making a list of all the friends you need to make contact with. Try making one date a week, going down the list until you've visited with each one. Some things you can do:

- When a friend works nearby, a quick lunch at a fast-food restaurant may be all you need to reconnect. But if you're not allowed an occasional extended lunch hour, the complications of such a meeting can be enormous and perhaps not worth the risk to your job.

- If your friend has children, you may opt for dinner at a family pizza restaurant that offers the children grand entertainment while giving adults an opportunity to talk. (Make sure your husband is taken care of before you leave, however.)

- Ask a friend to join you in the purchase of season tickets to a sports event or the theater. If your budget allows, a gift of such a ticket would be an especially thoughtful gesture.

- Keep a birthday book in which you list your friends' birthdays and other significant dates. Telephone or mail cards of best wishes on these days. One year a friend surprised me with a birthday gift of a small candle—handsomely wrapped and beribboned. It had been a long time since anyone outside of the family had remembered my birthday, and I was immensely pleased. The incident reminded me how meaningful unexpected friendship gifts can be. Such gifts are usually inexpensive items that are funny or reminders of good times you've shared as friends.

- When husbands are also acquainted and compatible, you can invite your friend's entire family to dinner. Hire a baby-sitter to look after both sets of children while the adults prepare dinner and enjoy being together.

Keep your efforts at maintaining friendships confined to your off-work hours. Remember, it is never appropriate for a friend to merely drop by your place of business. Since some of your friends are certain to be nonworking women and unfamiliar with this rule, arrange ahead of time for the receptionist to hold unexpected visitors in the reception area until you can come forward and explain the situation.

I love the Bible and want to study it and pray regularly, but there's never any time. How can I feed my spiritual hunger while juggling family, job, and church?

Good for you! This is what it's all about—what makes everything else fall into place. Recognizing the need for spiritual food puts you in an ideal starting position, but finding time alone with God requires a genuine dedicated commitment on the part of the working mother. It won't happen by itself. She must set aside a definite time and place in her life for meeting the Lord on a one-to-one basis.

There are probably hidden moments in your current schedule that could become your personal time with God. You'll also discover that a more streamlined, organized life (see chapter 4) will allow you greater flexibility for a morning or evening quiet time.

Prayer and Bible study require some uninterrupted time—at least fifteen minutes; but I also find it helpful to pause at my desk for a few minutes of silent prayer before beginning work each morning. A more in-depth talk with God can take place during the lunch hour or perhaps during an evening jog. Another secret: I like to keep Scripture cards and prayer lists in my purse. Sometimes the Scripture cards are purchased, sometimes handwritten from my private devotions; but they are always passages that speak to me and uplift me in a special way.

If concentrating on your talk with the Lord is difficult because of a fragmented or cluttered mind, try writing your prayers. Writing will help you pray more specifically. It is also a valuable tool for looking back and discovering where you've come from to date. A variation of the written prayer is the keeping of a concise prayer journal in which you list your prayer request, the date, and God's answer and the date. This, too, is a means of targeting your thoughts on specifics and can be exciting proof of God's interaction in your life when you look back and see how much he has done for you over a period of time.

Sometimes we want these special moments with God, but in the midst of go, go, go, we completely forget about taking that prearranged or hidden time to be alone with our Savior. To help us remember our goal, we can go on an occasional lunch fast. Drink fruit juices and read the Bible during this hour. (Plan on a slow afternoon and perhaps a carryout dinner from a fast-food restaurant for the family that night.)

Finally, follow a meaningful Bible study program that you can relate to. It's easy to become discouraged with Bible reading if it doesn't seem to correspond with today's problems and challenges. I enjoy Joyce Marie Smith's Bible studies (Tyndale House), which explore woman-centered topics and concerns.

Bibliography

Albrecht, Karl. *Executive Tune-up.* Englewood Cliffs, N.J.: Prentice-Hall, 1981.

Boston Women's Health Book Collective. *The New Our Bodies, Ourselves.* New York: Simon & Schuster, 1985.

Coffey, Barbara. *Glamour's Success Book.* New York: Simon & Schuster, 1983.

Curran, Dolores. *Traits of a Healthy Family.* Minneapolis: Winston Press, 1983.

David, Jay. *How to Play the Moonlighting Game.* New York: Facts on File, 1983.

Fanning, Robbie and Tony. *Get It All Done and Still Be Human.* Radnor, Penn.: Chilton, 1979.

Good Housekeeping. *101 Practical Ways to Make Money at Home.* New York: Good Housekeeping, 1971.

Home and School Institute. *Families Learning Together.* New York: Simon & Schuster, 1981.

Insel, Paul M., and Roth, Walton T. *Core Concepts in Health.* Palo Alto, Calif.: Mayfield, 1979.

Kilgo, Edith Flowers. *Money in the Cookie Jar.* Grand Rapids, Mich.: Baker, 1980.

Lasser, Jacob K. *How to Run a Small Business.* 5th ed. New York: McGraw-Hill, 1982.

Long, Lynette and Thomas. *The Handbook for*

Latchkey Children and Their Parents. New York: Arbor House, 1983.

Melton, David. *Survival Kit for Parents of Teenagers*. New York: St. Martin's, 1979.

Miller, Maureen. *Help Your Child for Life*. Niles, Ill.: Argus, 1978.

Novello, Joseph R. *Bringing Up Kids American Style*. New York: A & W, 1981.

Peale, Norman Vincent. *Positive Imaging*. Old Tappan, N.J.: Revell, 1981.

Pinkham, Mary Ellen. *Mary Ellen's Best of Helpful Hints, Book Two*. New York: Warner, 1981.

Posner, Mitchell. *Executive Essentials*. New York: Avon, 1982.

Rinella, R. and Robbins, C. *Career Power*. New York: American Management Association, 1980.

Ryglewicz, Hilary, and Thaler, Pat Koch. *Working Couples*. New York: Simon & Schuster, 1980.

Satir, Virginia M. *Peoplemaking*. Palo Alto, Calif.: Science and Behavior, 1972.

Urieli, Nachman, and Sernaque, Vivienne. *Part-Time Jobs*. New York: Ballantine, 1982.

Wallach, Janet. *Working Wardrobe*. Washington, D.C.: Acropolis, 1981.

Witt, Scott. *Second Income Money Makers*. West Nyack, N.Y.: Parker, 1975.

■ *Increase Your Personality Power* by Tim La-Haye. Why do you get angry? Afraid? Worried? Discover your unique personality type, then use it to live more effectively—at home, on the job, and under pressure. 72-1604-3 $2.25.

■ *Landing a Great Job* by Rodney S. Laughlin. Here are the essentials of a successful job hunt. Everything you need—from finding openings to closing interviews, and accepting offers. 72-2858-0 $2.25.

■ *The Perfect Way to Lose Weight* by Charles T. Kuntzleman and Daniel V. Runyon. Anyone can lose fat—and keep it off permanently. This tested program, developed by a leading physical fitness expert, shows how. 72-4935-9 $2.25.

■ *Strange Cults in America* by Bob Larson. An easy-reading update of six well-known cults: the Unification Church, Scientology, The Way International, Rajneesh, Children of God, and Transcendental Meditation. 72-6675-X $2.25.

■ *Surefire Ways to Beat Stress* by Don Osgood. A thought-provoking plan to help rid your life of unhealthy stress. Now you can tackle stress at its source—and win. 72-6693-8 $2.25.

■ *Temper Your Child's Tantrums* by Dr. James Dobson. You don't need to feel frustrated as a parent. The celebrated author and "Focus on the Family" radio host wants to give you the keys to firm, but loving, discipline in your home. 72-6994-5 $2.25.

■ *Terrific Tips for Parents* by Paul Lewis. The editor of *DADS ONLY* newsletter shares his findings on building character, confidence, and closeness at home. 72-7010-2 $2.25.

■ *When the Doctor Says, "It's Cancer"* by Mary Beth Moster. Cancer will strike approximately three out of four American families. Find out how to cope when you or someone you love hears this diagnosis. 72-7981-9 $2.25.

■ *When Your Friend Needs You* by Paul Welter. Do you know what to say when a friend comes to you for help? Here's how to express your care in an effective way. 72-7998-3 $2.25.